American Government

Test Pack

W285 v1.01

ISBN 978-0-8251-5630-4

J. Weston Walch, Publisher
P.O. Box 802 | Culver City, CA 90232
www.socialstudies.com/walch
Printed in the United States of America

Table of Contents

To the Teacher

Power Basics® is a complete textbook program designed to meet the needs of students who are daunted by traditional textbooks. *Power Basics* was created with the teacher in mind, as well. The test pack for each student text in the *Power Basics* program includes straightforward, accurate, and easy-to-score assessment tools.

Each test pack includes

- a pretest that covers all the material in the student text
- a comprehensive test for every unit of the student text
- a posttest for final testing and assessment after working through the entire student text
- an answer key and testing guidance for both teacher and student

With testing a critical component of a school's curriculum today, students need to learn test-taking skills. This *Power Basics* test pack provides not only tests related to the student text, but special reference sections devoted to the topic of testing. "Testing Students Who Do Not Test Well" helps you give all your students the tools they need to be successful test-takers. "Test-Taking Strategies for *Power Basics*" and "Strategies for Standardized Testing" give students useful information about preparing for the tests in this test pack and for high-stakes standardized tests. These sections include key strategies for approaching tests with confidence. You may want to distribute and discuss these test-preparation tools before the pretest.

Finally, a handy record-keeping form permits you to track your students' progress as they work through the *Power Basics* student text.

Everything you need for test success is right here in *Power Basics*!

Testing Students Who Do Not Test Well

There are many reasons why some students do not test well. There may be language barriers, learning differences, or a failure to perceive the relevance or importance of a given assessment.

When working with a group of students who do not test well, it is important to identify the causes for the problems and, when possible, to find individual solutions for particular students.

Students who are easily distracted or who have been diagnosed with ADD or ADHD may benefit from taking the test in a quieter, more restrictive atmosphere. Give such students the option of taking a test during a break period, such as a study hall or lunch period. If possible, provide study carrels in your classroom to minimize external distractions.

Students with a low level of English proficiency will benefit from either having the instructions translated into their native language, having translation materials on their desks during the test, or having a translator present. Such students will invariably need more time than others to complete a test.

For students who see no benefit to a given test, discuss the purposes and benefits of testing in general with them ahead of time. There will be tests in every area of the student's life, from taking the test to become a licensed driver to getting into the college or trade school of his or her choice. Test-taking is an important skill, one that will serve students well throughout life.

The work you do with your students on test preparation will provide them with the tools they need to master not only the tests in this course, but the tests they will face throughout their educational experiences and careers.

Test-Taking Strategies for *Power Basics*®

Tests are a part of life. Whether you're facing a test in the classroom, a standardized test, or even a driver's test, there are tools you can use to help you be successful. The best way to do well on a test is to pay attention in class and study the material. But you can also prepare in other ways. Knowing how the test is set up can help you approach the test with confidence.

Tests come in many formats. They will vary in their structure. Some tests may contain only one question format, such as multiple choice. Others may have true/false, matching, fill-in-the-blank, short-answer, or essay questions. Some tests may ask you to read a passage and then answer questions about it. Others may ask you to refer to or make a graph or a chart. No matter what types of questions the test contains, using specific strategies for each question type can help you be successful.

The tests for the *Power Basics* ® program often include multiple-choice questions. The following strategies can help you answer this type of question.

Multiple Choice

In multiple-choice questions, you read each question and choose the best answer out of two or more choices. These choices are usually labeled with the letters *a, b, c, d,* and *e,* depending on the number of choices. Use the following steps to help you answer multiple-choice questions.

- Read the directions very carefully. Some multiple-choice tests will ask you to select the *correct* answer, and others will ask you to select the *best* answer.
- Read the first part of the question very carefully. Look for negative words such as *not, never, except, unless,* and so forth.
- Answer each question in your mind before looking at the answer choices. Then read the answer choices before selecting an answer.
- After reading the choices, rule out the choices that are obviously incorrect. Then choose an answer from the remaining choices.

AMERICAN GOVERNMENT • PRETEST

Circle the letter of the correct answer to each of the following questions and statements.

1. Suppose a country has no leaders at all. Every citizen does as he or she pleases. This is an example of ______.
   a. democracy
   b. dictatorship
   c. anarchy
   d. monarchy

---

2. Suppose a country has been ruled by members of the same family for hundreds of years. This is an example of ______.
   a. democracy
   b. dictatorship
   c. anarchy
   d. monarchy

---

3. Suppose a country holds elections every year so that its citizens can vote on issues. This is an example of ______.
   a. democracy
   b. dictatorship
   c. anarchy
   d. monarchy

---

4. Suppose a country is run by a person who took power by force. This is an example of ______.
   a. democracy
   b. dictatorship
   c. anarchy
   d. monarchy

---

5. In a representative democracy, which leader would you expect to find?
   a. a despot who has a huge army
   b. a queen who has inherited power from her father
   c. a senator who has been elected by citizens
   d. a dictator who rules through fear

6. Suppose a state has 24 members in the House of Representatives. How many electors does this state have in the Electoral College?
   a. 2
   b. 22
   c. 24
   d. 26

---

7. What is an elector?
   a. a member of Congress
   b. anyone who works for the federal government
   c. a member of the Electoral College
   d. a citizen who votes in an election

---

8. What did the Executive Compromise involve?
   a. setting checks and balances
   b. limiting the power of the president
   c. deciding how states would be represented in Congress
   d. abolishing slavery

---

9. Which of the following is NOT a basic principle of the U.S. Constitution?
   a. inherent rights
   b. separation of powers
   c. self-government
   d. anarchy

---

10. Which of the following is an inherent right?
   a. freedom of speech
   b. the right to own property
   c. the right to a fair trial
   d. all the above

11. Congress is part of which branch of government?
    - a. executive
    - b. legislative
    - c. judicial
    - d. federal

---

12. The president is part of which branch of government?
    - a. executive
    - b. legislative
    - c. judicial
    - d. federal

---

13. What is one way for the president to check the power of the Supreme Court?
    - a. by appointing new justices to fill any openings on the court
    - b. by declaring that a court decision goes against the Constitution
    - c. by approving new salaries for justices
    - d. by impeaching a justice

---

14. Suppose you wanted to find out how bills are passed in the U.S. Congress. Which part of the Constitution would give you this information?
    - a. the Preamble
    - b. the articles
    - c. the amendments
    - d. the Bill of Rights

---

15. Suppose you wanted to find out about the right to own guns. Which part of the Constitution would give you this information?
    - a. the Preamble
    - b. the articles
    - c. the amendments
    - d. the Bill of Rights

16. What is a political party?

- **a.** a group of candidates for president
- **b.** a group of people who believe in democracy
- **c.** a group of people who stand for certain ideas
- **d.** a group of people who work in the same community

17. Which statement is TRUE about the U.S. political system?

- **a.** It has only one political party.
- **b.** It has two major political parties.
- **c.** It has no small political parties.
- **d.** It has many major political parties.

18. A government that has several political parties is most likely a(n) ______.

- **a.** anarchy
- **b.** dictatorship
- **c.** monarchy
- **d.** representative democracy

19. A government that has only one party is most likely a ______.

- **a.** dictatorship
- **b.** monarchy
- **c.** direct democracy
- **d.** representative democracy

20. Why do states require voter registration?

- **a.** to make sure that citizens do not vote more than once in any election
- **b.** so that citizens who register can vote early
- **c.** to keep track of population growth
- **d.** to keep track of how many people vote for each party

21. Which of the following is a responsibility of Congress?
    a. controlling trade
    b. borrowing money for government
    c. keeping up the armed services
    d. all of the above

---

22. Suppose a senator proposes a bill and the Senate finally passes it. What happens to the bill next?
    a. The bill becomes a law.
    b. The bill goes to the House of Representatives.
    c. The bill goes to the president.
    d. The bill goes to the Supreme Court.

---

23. Which of the following is NOT a duty of the vice president?
    a. breaking ties in the Senate
    b. taking part in cabinet meetings
    c. serving on the National Security Council
    d. serving as head of the armed forces

---

24. Which of the following would be tried in a civil case?
    a. a man accused of robbing a bank
    b. a woman accused of shoplifting jewelry
    c. a man accused of burning a building down on purpose
    d. a woman who is being sued by her neighbor over a property dispute

---

25. What is one way for the Supreme Court to check the power of Congress?
    a. by vetoing a bill passed by Congress
    b. by amending the Constitution
    c. by declaring that a bill passed by Congress goes against the Constitution
    d. by vetoing a law signed by the president

26. Which branch of government decides whether or not a law goes against the Constitution?

a. executive

b. legislative

c. judicial

d. federal

27. What is one objection to the Electoral College system?

a. It increases the chance of having a tie in the election.

b. It is not direct democracy.

c. It meets only once every four years.

d. It has trouble choosing a president.

28. When would the number of electors from a state increase?

a. when the state's population decreases

b. when the state's population remains the same

c. when the state's population is stable for 10 years

d. when the state's population increases

29. Which event comes right after the national conventions?

a. the primary elections

b. the general election

c. the presidential inauguration

d. the electoral vote

30. Which of the following should you NOT consider when learning about presidential candidates?

a. voting record

b. experience

c. looks

d. stand on the issues

31. What is the highest state court?

- **a.** the state supreme court
- **b.** appellate court
- **c.** general trial court
- **d.** circuit court

---

32. Which of the following is NOT a governor's duty?

- **a.** proposing federal laws
- **b.** carrying out state laws
- **c.** pardoning criminals convicted in state courts
- **d.** leading the state National Guard

---

33. What state officer is in charge of representing the state in court?

- **a.** the lieutenant governor
- **b.** the treasurer
- **c.** the secretary of state
- **d.** the attorney general

---

34. Which of the following is NOT a state service?

- **a.** keeping prices fair on gas
- **b.** making sure food is safe
- **c.** paying for citizens' electricity
- **d.** protecting natural resources

---

35. What is a sales tax?

- **a.** a charge on the goods people buy
- **b.** a charge on the money people make
- **c.** a charge on the money businesses make
- **d.** a charge on the value of land people own

36. What local laws protect people from robbery?
   a. theft laws
   b. vandalism laws
   c. traffic laws
   d. arson laws

---

37. What kind of municipal court handles minor cases?
   a. small-claims court
   b. juvenile court
   c. criminal court
   d. general trial court

---

38. What is the most common type of special district?
   a. water district
   b. school district
   c. public utility district
   d. sanitation district

---

39. In what building are county government offices located?
   a. the county seat
   b. the county courthouse
   c. the county ward
   d. the county system

---

40. What type of city government does NOT have a chief executive?
   a. the weak-mayor system
   b. the strong-mayor system
   c. the city manager system
   d. the city commission system

UNIT 1 TEST • WHAT IS GOVERNMENT?

Circle the letter of the correct answer to each of the following questions and statements.

1. A country with no elections, no leaders, and no rules is a(n) ______.
   a. democracy
   b. dictatorship
   c. anarchy
   d. monarchy

---

2. A country where every citizen votes on every decision is a(n) ______.
   a. direct democracy
   b. representative democracy
   c. moderate dictatorship
   d. extreme monarchy

---

3. Which of the following describes a totalitarian state?
   a. It is controlled by one leader who is not elected.
   b. It is run by one or more elected leaders.
   c. It is not run by anyone.
   d. It has fair elections once every four years.

---

4. Suppose a country has one ruler. This ruler has inherited her position from her mother. What type of government does this country have?
   a. a dictatorship
   b. a monarchy
   c. a democracy
   d. anarchy

---

5. What is one difference between a democracy and a dictatorship?
   a. A democracy gives every person a say, but a dictatorship does not.
   b. A dictatorship gives every person a say, but a democracy does not.
   c. Only a democracy has political parties.
   d. Only a democracy has rulers.

6. What is anarchy?
   a. a government with elected representatives
   b. a government with one ruler who uses force to stay in power
   c. the absence of rulers or government
   d. a government with one ruler who inherits power

---

7. What type of government would allow its citizens to vote their representatives out of office?
   a. a dictatorship
   b. anarchy
   c. a democracy
   d. a monarchy

---

8. In a direct democracy, citizens ______.
   a. have a say on every single issue, no matter how small
   b. do not have any voting rights
   c. vote for representatives to make decisions for them
   d. follow a strong ruler who makes all the decisions

---

9. A country controlled by a brutal leader who rules by force is a(n) _______.
   a. direct democracy
   b. representative democracy
   c. dictatorship
   d. anarchy

---

10. What is a monarchy?
   a. a government with elected representatives
   b. a government with one ruler who uses force to stay in power
   c. the absence of rulers or government
   d. a government with one ruler who inherits power

11. Which of the following is NOT true of a dictatorship?
    a. The people have little power over their lives.
    b. The people can choose their leaders.
    c. There is usually only one political party
    d. A strong ruler controls the government.

---

12. A country with two parties is most likely a(n) ______.
    a. anarchy
    b. dictatorship
    c. democracy
    d. monarchy

---

13. A country with only one party is most likely a(n) ______.
    a. anarchy
    b. dictatorship
    c. democracy
    d. monarchy

---

14. What type of government encourages political parties?
    a. extreme anarchy
    b. moderate dictatorship
    c. representative democracy
    d. moderate monarchy

---

15. Citizens in a town vote to give money to a new fire station. This is an example of ______.
    a. direct democracy
    b. representative democracy
    c. a totalitarian state
    d. an ancient monarchy

UNIT 2 TEST • THE CONSTITUTIONAL FRAMEWORK

Circle the letter of the correct answer to each of the following questions and statements.

1. What is the U.S. Constitution?

- **a.** the country's legislative branch
- **b.** the country's executive branch
- **c.** the Supreme Court
- **d.** the highest law of the land

---

2. The Articles of Confederation _____.

- **a.** argued for the right to form a new country
- **b.** explained the wrongs done by the English king
- **c.** were the first U.S. Constitution
- **d.** set up a strong national government

---

3. What was the result of the Great Compromise?

- **a.** a Congress with two houses
- **b.** a president who could veto laws
- **c.** a Supreme Court with nine justices
- **d.** a Bill of Rights

---

4. The Three-Fifths Compromise had to do with what issue?

- **a.** the presidency
- **b.** freedom of speech
- **c.** slavery
- **d.** inherent rights

---

5. The division of power between federal and state government is called _____.

- **a.** self-government
- **b.** federalism
- **c.** checks and balances
- **d.** separation of powers

6. Which part of the Constitution describes how the U.S. government works?
   a. the Preamble
   b. the articles
   c. the amendments
   d. the Bill of Rights

7. Which part of the Constitution protects citizens' freedom of speech?
   a. the Preamble
   b. the articles
   c. the amendments
   d. the Bill of Rights

8. A two-thirds vote of both houses of Congress is needed to _______.
   a. propose an amendment to the Constitution
   b. ratify an amendment to the Constitution
   c. veto a law passed by the president
   d. send an amendment back to the Senate

9. What was the problem with the Articles of Confederation?
   a. They did not give the federal government enough power.
   b. They gave the federal government too much power.
   c. They did now allow people to own their own property.
   d. They gave too much power to the Supreme Court.

10. The Constitutional Convention of 1787 decided on a legislature with two houses. What was this agreement called?
    a. the Great Compromise
    b. the Three-Fifths Compromise
    c. the Bill of Rights
    d. the Executive Compromise

11. The Constitutional Convention of 1787 worked out a compromise on slavery. What was this agreement called?
    a. the Great Compromise
    b. the Three-Fifths Compromise
    c. the Bill of Rights
    d. the Executive Compromise

12. What is federalism?
    a. the division of power between different branches of government
    b. the balancing of power between the three branches of government
    c. the right of all people to life, liberty, and the pursuit of happiness
    d. the division of power between national and state governments

13. What do the articles of the Constitution describe?
    a. how the U.S. government works
    b. the reasons for writing the Constitution
    c. the basic freedoms of all U.S. citizens
    d. the reasons for starting a new nation

14. What is the purpose of the Bill of Rights?
    a. to explain how the U.S. government works
    b. to describe why the Constitution was written
    c. to explain how to change the Constitution
    d. to protect the basic freedoms of all U.S. citizens

15. What is needed for Congress to override a presidential veto?
    a. a two-thirds vote of both houses of Congress
    b. a two-thirds vote of all senators
    c. a three-fourths vote of states' conventions
    d. the president's approval

UNIT 3 TEST • POLITICAL PARTIES AND VOTING

Circle the letter of the correct answer to each of the following questions and statements.

1. What was the purpose of the "voting amendments"?
   - a. to give more people the right to vote
   - b. to make sure people vote more often
   - c. to make sure people register to vote
   - d. to make sure political parties are honest

2. Keisha has just registered to vote. What does this mean?
   - a. She has chosen a candidate.
   - b. She has signed up to vote.
   - c. She has chosen a party.
   - d. She has decided not to vote.

3. What kind of political system does the United States have?
   - a. a one-party system
   - b. a two-party system
   - c. a system of many major political parties
   - d. The United States does not have any political parties.

4. What kind of political system does China have?
   - a. a one-party system
   - b. a two-party system
   - c. a multi-party system
   - d. China does not have any political parties.

5. Which one of the following is NOT eligible to vote in the United States?
   - a. a citizen who is over 75 years old
   - b. a citizen who reads poorly
   - c. a citizen who has no religion
   - d. a citizen who is under 18 years old

6. What is an independent voter?
   a. a person who votes for a candidate
   b. a person who belongs to a political party
   c. a person who does not believe in elections
   d. a person who does not belong to a political party

---

7. Which of the following is NOT a feature of a stable government?
   a. It is orderly.
   b. Work gets done.
   c. It changes every few months.
   d. Citizens are satisfied.

---

8. In a representative democracy, political parties ______.
   a. are encouraged
   b. are not encouraged
   c. are not allowed
   d. do not represent minorities

---

9. Which of the following is an example of representative democracy?
   a. Citizens vote to give money to a highway project.
   b. Citizens vote not to give money to a highway project.
   c. A ruler decides to give money to a highway project.
   d. Citizens vote for a senator who promises to give money to a highway project.

---

10. Each person below is an American citizen. Which one is NOT allowed to vote?
   a. a 17-year-old Asian student
   b. a 20-year-old Jewish man
   c. a 54-year-old homeless man
   d. a 72-year-old retired teacher

11. Voter registration prevents citizens from _____.

a. voting twice in the same election

b. voting for an independent party candidate

c. voting for state representatives

d. voting without paying attention to the issues

---

12. What is a group of parties that band together for more power?

a. a democracy

b. a one-party system

c. a multi-party system

d. a coalition

---

13. A voter who does not choose a party is a(n) _____.

a. independent voter

b. member of the Republican Party

c. member of the Democratic Party

d. monarchist

---

14. Which of the following countries has a multi-party system?

a. Italy

b. Canada

c. the United States

d. Cuba

---

15. A stalemate can occur when which of the following happens?

a. A coalition is formed.

b. A compromise is reached.

c. A compromise is not reached, and nothing gets done.

d. The U.S. government passes a budget.

NAME: DATE:

UNIT 4 TEST • THE FEDERAL GOVERNMENT

Circle the letter of the correct answer to each of the following questions and statements.

1. What is the main duty of the executive branch?
   a. carrying out laws
   b. passing laws
   c. making laws
   d. interpreting laws

---

2. Which branch of government is Congress?
   a. executive
   b. legislative
   c. judicial
   d. constitutional

---

3. Which of the following is an executive check on the legislative branch?
   a. the legislature's power to override the president's veto
   b. the president's power to veto a law passed by Congress
   c. the Supreme Court's power to say that a law is not constitutional
   d. the president's power to appoint justices to the Supreme Court

---

4. What is the supreme law of the United States?
   a. Congress
   b. the president
   c. the Constitution
   d. the legislature

---

5. Separation of powers ensures that _____.
   a. the president carries out laws
   b. decisions of the Supreme Court are final
   c. Congress deals with budgets and taxes
   d. no branch of government has too much power

6. What does it mean when a president vetoes a bill passed by Congress?
    a. The president approves the bill.
    b. The president asks for more information.
    c. The president passes the bill to the vice president.
    d. The president refuses to sign the bill.

7. Which branch of government interprets laws?
    a. executive
    b. legislative
    c. judicial
    d. constitutional

8. The Supreme Court has the power to say that a law passed by Congress is not constitutional. What is this an example of?
    a. a legislative check on the judicial branch
    b. an executive check on the legislative branch
    c. an executive check on the judicial branch
    d. a judicial check on the legislative branch

9. Who are the leaders of Congress?
    a. the president and vice president
    b. senators and representatives
    c. justices and judges
    d. electors

10. What does it mean when Congress overrides a president's veto?
    a. Congress accepts the veto without question.
    b. Congress votes to set the veto aside and passes the law anyway.
    c. Congress takes the bill to the Supreme Court.
    d. Congress sits down with the president to debate the bill.

11. Why do we say that our Congress is "bicameral"?

- **a.** because it has two main parts
- **b.** because it is part of the federal government
- **c.** because of separation of powers
- **d.** because of federalism

---

12. What is the lowest-level federal court?

- **a.** the Supreme Court
- **b.** circuit court
- **c.** district court
- **d.** general trial court

---

13. What is the second-highest federal court?

- **a.** the Supreme Court
- **b.** circuit court
- **c.** district court
- **d.** trial court

---

14. What is a precedent?

- **a.** a discussion held in Congress
- **b.** a ruling made by judges in the past
- **c.** an overturned verdict
- **d.** a law declared unconstitutional by the Supreme Court

---

15. What is the first step in passing a bill?

- **a.** A committee researches the bill.
- **b.** A senator or representative introduces the bill to Congress.
- **c.** The president approves the bill.
- **d.** A committee recommends the bill.

UNIT 5 TEST • THE PRESIDENTIAL ELECTION PROCESS

Circle the letter of the correct answer to each of the following questions.

1. Whom do voters choose in a primary election?
   a. a representative for Congress
   b. a senator
   c. the president of the United States
   d. a presidential candidate from their political party

2. Which of the following comes first in the presidential election process?
   a. the general election
   b. the primary elections
   c. the national conventions
   d. the presidential inauguration

3. During which of the following do the people of the country vote in a presidential election?
   a. the primary elections
   b. the national conventions
   c. the general election
   d. the presidential inauguration

4. Suppose a state has 15 members in the House of Representatives. How many electors does this state have in the Electoral College?
   a. 15
   b. 17
   c. 30
   d. 32

5. The Electoral College system is an example of which type of government?
   a. monarchy
   b. dictatorship
   c. direct democracy
   d. representative democracy

6. What would happen if a state's population increased?
   a. Its number of electors would decrease.
   b. Its number of electors would increase.
   c. Its number of electors would stay the same.
   d. The number of electors is determined by the number of senators, not by population.

---

7. What is the purpose of a primary election?
   a. to elect a senator
   b. to elect a representative
   c. to choose presidential candidates
   d. to choose electors

---

8. Suppose a presidential candidate wins a state's popular vote. How many of the state's electoral votes does he or she get?
   a. It depends on the size of the win.
   b. It depends on the number of candidates in the race.
   c. The candidate gets at least half of the state's electoral votes.
   d. The candidate usually gets all of the state's electoral votes.

---

9. Which of the following comes last in the presidential election process?
   a. the primary elections
   b. the national conventions
   c. the general election
   d. the presidential inauguration

---

10. Suppose a state has 24 members in Congress. How many electors would this state have in the Electoral College?
   a. 12
   b. 24
   c. 26
   d. 30

11. What effect would a decrease in a state's population have on its number of electors?
    a. Its number of electors would decrease.
    b. Its number of electors would increase.
    c. Its number of electors would stay the same.
    d. The number of electors is determined by the number of senators, not by population.

12. What are the special elections held to choose presidential candidates?
    a. general elections
    b. primary elections
    c. national elections
    d. presidential elections

13. What does it mean when a presidential candidate gets all of a state's electoral votes?
    a. He or she won that state's popular vote.
    b. He or she won that state's popular vote by a large margin.
    c. He or she won that state's popular vote by a small margin.
    d. He or she will become president of the United States.

14. What would happen if no presidential candidate received a majority of the electoral vote?
    a. The Electoral College would vote again.
    b. The American people would vote again.
    c. The House of Representatives would choose the winner.
    d. The Supreme Court would vote for a winner.

15. What are "sound bites"?
    a. short, interesting statements made by candidates that will play well in news reports
    b. painful bursts of noise
    c. pieces of information spread by a computer virus
    d. none of the above

UNIT 6 TEST • STATE GOVERNMENT

Circle the letter of the correct answer to each of the following questions and statements.

1. Which of the following powers belong to state government?
   a. overseeing state transportation
   b. overseeing the state police
   c. overseeing state businesses
   d. all the above

2. What state court tries criminal cases?
   a. appellate courts
   b. state supreme courts
   c. lower courts
   d. general trial courts

3. Which of the following is NOT a state service?
   a. cleaning up national parks
   b. running state colleges
   c. running state hospitals
   d. cleaning up state highways

4. Which of the following is a charge on the value of land people own?
   a. sales tax
   b. property tax
   c. income tax
   d. corporate tax

5. What is an initiative?
   a. a vote on a special issue
   b. a vote by the state legislature
   c. a special vote to remove someone from office
   d. a vote on a proposed solution to a problem after a petition

6. What state officer manages state money?
   a. the governor
   b. the attorney general
   c. the secretary of state
   d. the treasurer

---

7. What state officer proposes state laws?
   a. the governor
   b. the attorney general
   c. the secretary of state
   d. the treasurer

---

8. Repairing a state bridge is an example of a(n) ______.
   a. ordinance
   b. toll
   c. public work
   d. consumer protection service

---

9. Which of the following powers does NOT belong to state government?
   a. making state laws
   b. setting state taxes
   c. running the U.S. army
   d. running the state police

---

10. Which types of cases do the lowest state courts handle?
   a. murders
   b. robberies
   c. cases that involve traffic violations
   d. all criminal cases

11. Which of the following is a state service?

- **a.** protecting consumers from unsafe food
- **b.** building national highways
- **c.** cleaning up national parks
- **d.** settling disputes between states

---

12. What is an income tax?

- **a.** a charge on the money people make
- **b.** a charge on the land people own
- **c.** a charge on the things people buy
- **d.** a charge on the money businesses make

---

13. What is the term for a vote held to remove someone from office?

- **a.** initiative
- **b.** referendum
- **c.** recall
- **d.** petition

---

14. Which of the following is NOT a duty of the governor?

- **a.** passing state laws
- **b.** working with legislators
- **c.** suggesting state laws
- **d.** carrying out state laws

---

15. Charging people to use a state highway is an example of a(n) _____.

- **a.** ordinance
- **b.** public work
- **c.** toll
- **d.** consumer protection service

NAME: DATE:

UNIT 7 TEST • LOCAL GOVERNMENT

Circle the letter of the correct answer to each of the following questions and statements.

1. What is the largest unit of local government?
   - a. city government
   - b. state government
   - c. village government
   - d. county government

---

2. What is the term for a voting area in a city?
   - a. public work
   - b. special district
   - c. city ward
   - d. county court house

---

3. Who puts together the city budget in a weak-mayor system?
   - a. the city council
   - b. the state legislature
   - c. the mayor
   - d. the city manager

---

4. What local laws keep people from setting fires on purpose?
   - a. theft laws
   - b. vandalism laws
   - c. traffic laws
   - d. arson laws

---

5. What type of municipal court handles cases that involve people under 18?
   - a. criminal court
   - b. traffic court
   - c. small-claims court
   - d. juvenile court

6. Which of the following is NOT an example of a special district?
   a. a public utility district
   b. a sanitation district
   c. a toll district
   d. a water district

---

7. What happens when a state grants home rule to a local government?
   a. The state allows local government to decide all local matters.
   b. The state runs the city council.
   c. The state advises representatives in local government.
   d. The state runs the county courthouse.

---

8. Which of the following is the smallest unit of local government?
   a. city government
   b. state government
   c. village government
   d. county government

---

9. What is a city ward?
   a. a city where county government is located
   b. a city where state government is located
   c. a building where county government is located
   d. a voting area in a city

---

10. The city council's power is weak in a ______.
   a. weak-mayor system
   b. strong-mayor system
   c. city manager system
   d. small city

11. What local laws stop people from destroying the property of others?
    a. health codes
    b. traffic laws
    c. vandalism laws
    d. theft laws

12. What type of municipal court handles matters that involve parking tickets?
    a. divorce court
    b. traffic court
    c. small-claims court
    d. juvenile court

13. Which of the following is NOT an example of a special district?
    a. a water district
    b. a district court
    c. a public utility district
    d. a school district

14. What happens if a state decides to take home rule away from its counties?
    a. The counties would have less power.
    b. The counties would have more power.
    c. The counties would have about the same amount of power.
    d. The counties would be run by the federal government.

15. Which of the following is NOT an example of a local protective service?
    a. police department
    b. national defense
    c. fire department
    d. garbage collection

AMERICAN GOVERNMENT • POSTTEST

Circle the letter of the correct answer to each of the following questions and statements.

1. In an anarchy, there is ______.

a. a dictator who took power by force
b. a king who inherited power
c. an elected senator
d. no ruler at all

---

2. What kind of leader would you expect to find in a monarchy?

a. a dictator who took power by force
b. a king who inherited power
c. an elected senator
d. no ruler at all

---

3. Which form of government gives all citizens a voice in government?

a. democracy
b. dictatorship
c. anarchy
d. monarchy

---

4. In a dictatorship, what kind of leader would you expect to find?

a. a ruler who took power by force
b. a king who inherited power
c. an elected senator
d. no ruler at all

---

5. Which form of government has its citizens elect representatives?

a. representative democracy
b. extreme dictatorship
c. moderate anarchy
d. direct democracy

6. What does the legislative branch of government do?
   a. hears cases in court
   b. enforces the nation's laws
   c. passes new laws for the country
   d. decides how much power the president and the Supreme Court can have

---

7. The Supreme Court has the power to do which of the following?
   a. override the president's veto
   b. veto the president's budget
   c. appoint their own justices
   d. strike down a law passed by Congress

---

8. The president has the power to do which of the following?
   a. stop the actions of the Supreme Court
   b. appoint Supreme Court justices
   c. override a veto from Congress
   d. introduce new bills in the Senate

---

9. A member of the Electoral College is a(n) ______.
   a. mayor
   b. justice
   c. senator
   d. elector

---

10. Which of the following is NOT a basic principle of the U.S. Constitution?
   a. inherent rights
   b. separation of powers
   c. self-government
   d. monarchy

11. What issue did the Three-Fifths Compromise involve?

a. checks and balances

b. the powers of the president

c. freedom of the press

d. slavery

---

12. Which of the following is an inherent right?

a. freedom of religion

b. freedom of speech

c. right to a fair trial

d. all the above

---

13. What do the articles of the Constitution describe?

a. the right of citizens to voice their opinions freely

b. the way bills are passed in Congress

c. the right of citizens to vote, regardless of their race

d. the purpose of the Constitution

---

14. What does the Bill of Rights describe?

a. the right of citizens to voice their opinions freely

b. the way bills are passed in Congress

c. the setup of the executive branch

d. the purpose of the Constitution

---

15. What was the result of the Executive Compromise?

a. The president was allowed to veto bills from Congress.

b. Slaves would not be counted as taxable property.

c. Congress would have two chambers, or parts.

d. A president's term could last only four years.

16. How many major political parties is a dictatorship likely to have?

a. zero or one

b. two

c. three

d. more than three

---

17. Which of the following countries has a two-party system?

a. Cuba

b. China

c. Canada

d. Iraq

---

18. How many major political parties does the United States have?

a. zero or one

b. two

c. twenty

d. more than twenty

---

19. How are citizens kept from voting twice in an election?

a. They must sign up for a political party before voting.

b. They must serve jury duty before voting.

c. They must register to vote in advance.

d. They are expected to follow the honor system.

---

20. When do voters choose presidential candidates from their political parties?

a. during the general election

b. during the national election

c. at the presidential inauguration

d. during the primary elections

21. What does the judicial branch of government do?

- **a.** It makes and passes laws.
- **b.** It says whether a law is constitutional.
- **c.** It enforces, or carries out, laws.
- **d.** It gives Congress advice about laws.

---

22. Who are the heads of the executive branch of government?

- **a.** the justices of the Supreme Court
- **b.** the Cabinet
- **c.** the senators and representatives
- **d.** the president and vice president

---

23. Who has the power to borrow money for the government?

- **a.** the president
- **b.** the vice president
- **c.** Congress
- **d.** the Supreme Court

---

24. Who is responsible for breaking any ties in the Senate?

- **a.** the president
- **b.** the vice president
- **c.** Congress
- **d.** the Supreme Court

---

25. Suppose the president signs a bill. What happens to the bill next?

- **a.** The bill becomes a law.
- **b.** The bill goes to the House of Representatives.
- **c.** The bill goes to the Supreme Court.
- **d.** The bill goes to the Senate for changes.

26. Which of the following would be handled in a civil case?

a. a man accused of shooting his boss

b. a woman accused of kidnapping a baby

c. a man accused of stealing a television

d. a woman being sued by her neighbor for dumping trash in his yard

---

27. What is one argument in favor of the Electoral College?

a. It has results that are clear.

b. It is not direct democracy.

c. It meets every four years.

d. It has trouble choosing a president.

---

28. Suppose a state has 33 members in the House of Representatives. How many electors would this state have in the Electoral College?

a. 17

b. 33

c. 35

d. 66

---

29. What happens if a state's population increases?

a. Its number of electors decreases.

b. Its number of electors stays the same.

c. Its number of electors always increases by two.

d. Its number of electors increases.

---

30. Which event comes right before the national conventions?

a. the primary elections

b. the general election

c. the presidential inauguration

d. the electoral vote

31. Which of the following is the highest state court?

a. the state supreme court

b. appellate court

c. general trial court

d. circuit court

---

32. What state officer heads the state National Guard?

a. the secretary of state

b. the treasurer

c. the attorney general

d. the governor

---

33. Which of the following is NOT a state service?

a. keeping advertisements honest

b. making sure state parks are clean

c. helping citizens pay for heat

d. repairing a state bridge

---

34. What is a corporate tax?

a. a charge on the goods people buy

b. a charge on the money people make

c. a charge on the money businesses make

d. a charge on the value of land people own

---

35. What state officer represents the state in court?

a. the lieutenant governor

b. the treasurer

c. the secretary of state

d. the attorney general

36. What local laws help to prevent automobile accidents?

a. vandalism laws

b. arson laws

c. theft laws

d. traffic laws

---

37. What types of cases are handled by small-claims courts?

a. cases involving small sums of money

b. cases involving people under 18 years of age

c. cases involving rules of the road

d. cases involving the end of marriages

---

38. Which type of city government is likely to have no chief executive?

a. a weak-mayor system

b. a strong-mayor system

c. a city manager system

d. a city commission system

---

39. What is a special district?

a. an area of wealthy neighborhoods

b. an area set up to provide a special service

c. a voting area in a city

d. an area set up to manage schools

---

40. What does the county courthouse usually hold?

a. all county government offices

b. all legislative offices of the county

c. all judicial offices of the county

d. all executive offices of the county

Answer Key

Pretest

1. c	11. b	21. d	31. a
2. d	12. a	22. b	32. a
3. a	13. a	23. d	33. d
4. b	14. b	24. d	34. c
5. c	15. d	25. c	35. a
6. d	16. c	26. c	36. a
7. c	17. b	27. b	37. a
8. b	18. d	28. d	38. b
9. d	19. a	29. b	39. b
10. d	20. a	30. c	40. d

Unit 1 Test: What Is Government?

1. c	6. c	11. b
2. a	7. c	12. c
3. a	8. a	13. b
4. b	9. c	14. c
5. a	10. d	15. a

Unit 2 Test: The Constitutional Framework

1. d	6. b	11. b
2. c	7. d	12. d
3. a	8. a	13. a
4. c	9. a	14. d
5. d	10. a	15. a

Unit 3 Test: Political Parties and Voting

1. a	6. d	11. a
2. b	7. c	12. d
3. b	8. a	13. a
4. a	9. d	14. a
5. d	10. a	15. c

Unit 4 Test: The Federal Government

1. a	6. d	11. a
2. b	7. c	12. c
3. b	8. d	13. b
4. c	9. b	14. b
5. d	10. b	15. b

Unit 5 Test: The Presidential Election Process

1. d	6. b	11. a
2. b	7. c	12. b
3. c	8. d	13. a
4. b	9. d	14. c
5. d	10. b	15. a

Unit 6 Test: State Government

1. d	6. d	11. a
2. d	7. a	12. a
3. a	8. c	13. c
4. b	9. c	14. a
5. d	10. c	15. c

Unit 7 Test: Local Government

1. d	6. c	11. c
2. c	7. a	12. b
3. a	8. c	13. b
4. d	9. d	14. a
5. d	10. b	15. b

Posttest

1. d	11. d	21. b	31. a
2. b	12. d	22. d	32. d
3. a	13. b	23. c	33. c
4. a	14. a	24. b	34. c
5. a	15. d	25. a	35. d
6. c	16. a	26. d	36. d
7. d	17. c	27. a	37. a
8. b	18. b	28. c	38. d
9. d	19. c	29. d	39. b
10. d	20. d	30. a	40. a

Student Record-Keeping Form

	Student Name	Student ID	Class Period	Pretest Score	Unit ___ Score	Unit ___ Score	Unit ___ Score	Unit ___ Score	Unit ___ Score	Unit ___ Score	Unit ___ Score	Unit ___ Score
1.												
2.												
3.												
4.												
5.												
6.												
7.												
8.												
9.												
10.												
11.												
12.												
13.												
14.												
15.												
16.												
17.												
18.												
19.												
20.												
21.												
22.												
23.												
24.												
25.												
26.												
27.												
28.												
29.												
30.												

Strategies for Standardized Testing

Test-taking is a skill. Just as you learn about forms of government, you can learn to succeed on standardized tests. State standardized tests are intended to measure your understanding of state and national curriculum standards. Of course, the best preparation for these exams is attention and participation in your daily classroom lessons.

Tests will vary in their structure and content. Some tests will contain multiple-choice questions with four answers, some with five. You might be required to write a long essay, or a series of short answers, or both. Whatever the structure of your specific exam, there are some general strategies you can use in order to test your best.

Know the Test

One of the most important things you can do to prepare for a test is to become familiar with it in advance. If your teacher has sample tests or questions, these are the best resources for you to use for practice. You will feel more confident on test day if you are already familiar with the directions. If you open your test booklet to see a set of directions you've worked with before, you won't have to spend valuable test time learning them.

Knowing the exam will also prepare you for the way particular standards are tested. Make sure there are few surprises on test day by knowing in advance what types of question to expect.

It's Your Test

Once you sit down with the test booklet, it's your test. You decide your approach to individual questions. Some people, for example, would rather answer a question before looking at the answer choices. Others like to scan the choices before attempting to answer. Whichever approach makes you feel more comfortable and confident is the right approach for you.

The challenge on these exams is not just answering the questions, but answering them in the allotted time. It's important to pace yourself so that you have time to finish each section and preferably have some time left to check your work. Generally, you are allotted a specific amount of time for each particular section. Within each section, the order in which you approach the questions is up to you. If you encounter an item that gives you trouble, you can skip it and return to it later. Circle these questions in your test booklet so that you can quickly and easily find them. If you do skip questions or move around in a section, be extra careful that you're filling in your answers next to the right question numbers on your answer sheet.

Strategies for Standardized Testing, *cont.*

On most tests, you're free to mark up your test booklet. In addition to circling questions you skip, you might want to mark questions you're unsure about. Those can be the first questions you revisit if you have any time left at the end of a section. You can also underline important information in reading passages, cross out answer choices you've eliminated, and so forth.

Making Choices

If your exam doesn't deduct points for wrong answers, it's a good idea to fill in an answer for every question. Even if there is a wrong answer penalty, making an educated guess can improve your score. Many questions on state standardized exams are in multiple-choice format. You might understand enough about a question to eliminate one or more of its answer choices. If so, you dramatically increase your odds of selecting the correct answer from the remaining choices.

It is always important to read each question carefully to make sure you're doing exactly what it asks. Not every multiple-choice question asks you to choose the one correct response. In other words, you might be asked to select the one incorrect choice or to decide whether all of the choices are correct.

Some key words to look out for in multiple-choice questions are:

- sometimes/always/never
- except
- all of the above
- synonym/antonym
- same/opposite

The foundation for success on your test is the content you learn in your classroom. Using some basic strategies and doing practice tests will also help you get ready for test time. Follow the formula for success below, and you can be confident that you'll do your best on test day.

classroom knowledge + strategic insight + practice = SUCCESS

Strategies for Standardized Testing, *cont.*

Here are some additional hints to help you succeed on any standardized test.

Helpful Hints

1. Listen carefully to all instructions from the person giving the test.

2. Read directions carefully. Be sure you understand all the directions before beginning that section of the test.

3. Read each question carefully. Then read all the answer choices before you answer the question.

4. If it's taking you a lot of time to answer one question, move on to the next one. If you take too much time on one question, you may not have a chance to get through the whole test. Answer the questions you know first. Then go back to the others if you have time.

5. Be sure to mark your answers on the answer sheet that comes with the test booklet. You will probably be asked to shade the circle that contains the letter of your answer.

6. Take care when marking your answer sheet. Check to make sure that the number on the answer sheet matches the number of the question you are answering.

7. Since most standardized tests are scored by a machine, mark your answer clearly and darkly. Make sure you mark only one answer for each question.

8. If you have time, go back and check your answers.